The Colors We Eat

Pink Foods

Isabel Thomas

Heinemann Library
Chicago, Illinois

© 2005 Heinemann Library
a division of Reed Elsevier Inc.
Chicago, Illinois

Customer Service   888–454–2279
Visit our website at www.heinemannlibrary.com

Printed and bound in China by South China Printing Co. Ltd.

09 08 07 06 05
10 9 8 7 6 5 4 3 2 1

Library of Congress Cataloging-in-Publication Data
Thomas, Isabel, 1980-
    Pink foods / Isabel Thomas.
        p. cm. -- (The colors we eat)
    Includes index.
    ISBN 1-4034-6314-X (hc) -- ISBN 1-4034-6321-2 (pbk.)
    1. Food--Juvenile literature. 2. Pink--Juvenile literature. I. Title.
    TX355.T4528 2004
    641.3--dc22

                                    2004005218

Acknowledgments
The author and publisher are grateful to the following for permission to reproduce copyright material:
pp. 4, 5, 6, 7, 8, 12, 13, 14, 15, 16, 17, 18, 19, 20, 21, 21 Tudor Photography/Heinemann Library; p. 9 Ian Macguire; p. 10 Macduff Everton/Corbis; p. 11 Inga Spence/Holt Studios; 23 (cacti) Cumulus/Holt Studios.

Cover photograph: Tudor Photography/Heinemann Library.

Every effort has been made to contact copyright holders of any material reproduced in this book. Any omissions will be rectified in subsequent printings if notice is given to the publisher.

Special thanks to our advisory panel for their help in the preparation of this book:

Alice Bethke,
Library Consultant
Palo Alto, CA

Eileen Day,
Preschool Teacher
Chicago, IL

Sandra Gilbert,
Library Media Specialist
Fiest Elementary School
Houston, TX

Jan Gobeille,
Kindergarten Teacher
Garfield Elementary
Oakland, CA

Angela Leeper,
Educational Consultant
Wake Forest, NC

Melinda Murphy,
Library Media Specialist
Houston, TX

Some words are shown in bold, **like this.**
You can find them in the glossary on page 23.

Contents

Have You Eaten Pink Foods?

Colors are all around us.

You might have eaten some of these colors.

There are pink vegetables and fruits.

There are other pink foods, too.

What Are Some Big and Small Pink Foods?

Some foods are big and pink.

Watermelons are big, pink fruits.

Some foods are small and pink.

These beans are pink.

What Are Some Pink Fruits?

These are grapefruits.

Some grapefruits are pink inside.

A guava is a fruit.

The pink part of a guava is called the **flesh**.

Which Foods Have Pink Skins?

Garlic is a plant with pink skin.

People use garlic to add **flavor** to food.

Lychees are small, round fruits.

They have a bumpy, pink skin.

What Are Some Sweet Pink Foods?

Marshmallows are soft and fluffy.

They taste very sweet.

This is strawberry yogurt.

The red strawberries have turned
the yogurt pink.

Have You Tried These Pink Foods?

Shrimp are a kind of **seafood**.

They turn pink when they are cooked.

sandwich

ham

Ham is pink.

Some people use ham to make **sandwiches**.

What Are Some Strange Pink Foods?

Pitahayas are fruits with a bright pink shell.

Pitahayas grow on **cacti**.

Rhubarb is a plant.

You have to cook rhubarb **stalks** before you can eat them.

What Are Some Pink Drinks?

Pink lemonade is made from water, lemon juice, sugar, and cranberry juice.

The red cranberry juice turns the liquid pink!

This is pink grapefruit juice.

Try making your own by squeezing pink grapefruits.

Pink Mousse Recipe

Ask an adult to help you.

Mix up some strawberry jelly and pour in a can of evaporated milk.

Now whisk the mixture until
it is fluffy.

Leave the mousse in a cold fridge.

You can put marshmallows on
top before you eat it.

Quiz

Do you know what these pink foods are called?

Look for the answers on page 24.

Picture Glossary

cactus

page 16

spiky plant that grows in hot, dry places

flavor

page 10

what something tastes like

flesh

page 9

soft insides of a fruit

sandwich

page 15

two slices of bread with a filling

seafood

page 14

food that comes from the sea such as fish or shrimp

stalk

page 17

part of a plant that joins the flowers and roots together

Note to Parents and Teachers

Reading for information is an important part of a child's literacy development. Learning begins with a question about something. Help children think of themselves as investigators and researchers by encouraging their questions about the world around them. Each chapter in this book begins with a question. Read the question together. Look at the pictures. Talk about what you think the answer might be. Then read the text to find out if your predictions were correct. Think of other questions you could ask about the topic, and discuss where you might find the answers. Assist children in using the picture glossary and the index to practice new vocabulary and research skills.

Index

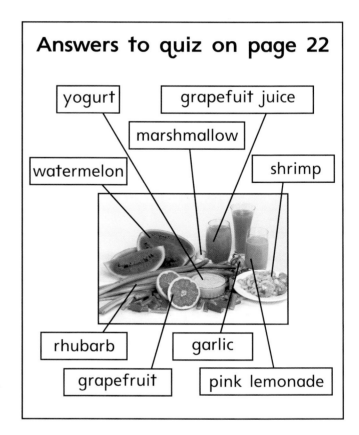

Answers to quiz on page 22

yogurt · grapefuit juice · marshmallow · watermelon · shrimp · rhubarb · grapefruit · garlic · pink lemonade